Yukon

Adrianna Morganelli

D0685363

Scholastic Canada Ltd.

Toronto New York London Auckland Sydney
Mexico City New Delhi Hong Kong Buenos Aires

Visual Credits

Cover: Paul Nicklen/National Geographic Stock; p. III: Michael Melford/National Geographic Stock; p. IV: iStockPhoto.com (top left), Harry Taylor/Dorling Kindersley (middle), David Walkins/Shutterstock (top right); p. 3: Mike Grandmaison/First Light (top), iStockPhoto.com (bottom); p. 4 : Mira/Alamy; p. 5: iStockPhoto.com (bottom left and right); p. 6: John Sylvester/AllCanadaPhotos.com; p. 7 and back cover: Randolph Images/Alamy; p. 8: Eric Gevaert/Shutterstock; p. 9: Outdoorsman/Dreamstime.com; p. 10: Michael DeYoung/Corbis; p. 11: Richard Hartmier/First Light; p. 12: Dbvirago/Dreamstime.com; p. 13: McCord Museum (top and bottom), iStockphoto.com (middle); p. 14: McCord Museum (top), Bettmann/Corbis (bottom); p. 15: Private Collection/The Bridgeman Art Library (top), Library and Archives Canada (inset); p. 16: Photoresearchers/First Light; p. 17: Glenbow Archives (top), The Granger Collection (bottom); p. 18: The Bridgeman Art Library; p. 19: Glenbow Archives; p. 20: William Kaye Lamb/Library and Archives Canada; p. 21: Yukon Archives/R.A. Cartter fonds/YA#1479; p. 22: Glenbow Archives; p. 23: Robert Postma/First Light; p. 24: Look and Learn/The Bridgeman Art Library; p. 25: The Granger Collection; p. 26: Peter Newark American Pictures/The Bridgeman Art Library; p. 27: Glenbow Archives (top), Pep Roig/Alamy (bottom); p. 28: Glenbow Archives; p. 29: Gunter Marx/Alamy (top), Library and Archives Canada (bottom); p. 30: Tom McNemar/Shutterstock (top), Pat Morrow/First Light (bottom); p. 31: James Marshall/Corbis (top), Pat Morrow/First Light (bottom); p. 32: Pat Morrow/First Light; p. 33: Vera Bogaerts/Shutterstock (top), Krasowit/Shutterstock (bottom); p. 34: Adam Barnard/Shutterstock (left), Peter Barrett/Shutterstock (right); p. 35: Paul Nicklen/National Geographic Stock; p. 36: AirScapes/Wayne Towriss; p. 37: Pictures Canada/First Light (top), Paul Nicklen/National Geographic Stock (bottom); p. 38: imagebroker/Alamy; p. 39: Material from *The Cremation of Sam McGee*, written by Robert Service, paintings by Ted Harrison is used by permission of Kids Can Press Ltd., Toronto. Illustration © 1986 Ted Harrison.; p. 40: Pat Morrow/First Light; p. 41: iStockPhoto.com (middle left), Cameramanz/Shutterstock (top), Iwka/Shutterstock (middle right), Robert Postma/First Light (bottom); p. 42: Kerry L. Werry/Shutterstock; p. 43: Glenbow Archives (top), Mike Slaughter/Torstar Photos (middle).

Produced by Plan B Book Packagers
Editorial: Ellen Rodger
Design: Rosie Gowsell-Pattison
Editor: Carrie Gleason
Special thanks to consultant and editor Terrance Cox, adjunct professor, Brock University;
Nancy Hodgson, Tanya Rutledge, Jim Chernishenko

Library and Archives Canada Cataloguing in Publication

Morganelli, Adrianna, 1979-
Yukon / by Adrianna Morganelli.
(Canada close up)
Includes index.
ISBN 978-0-545-98910-7
1. Yukon Territory--Juvenile literature.
I. Title. II. Series: Canada close up (Toronto, Ont.)
FC4011.2.M67 2009   j971.91   C2009-901797-0

ISBN-10 0-545-98910-8

Copyright © 2009 Scholastic Canada Ltd.
All rights reserved.

6 5 4 3 2   Printed in Canada 119   10 11 12 13 14

Contents

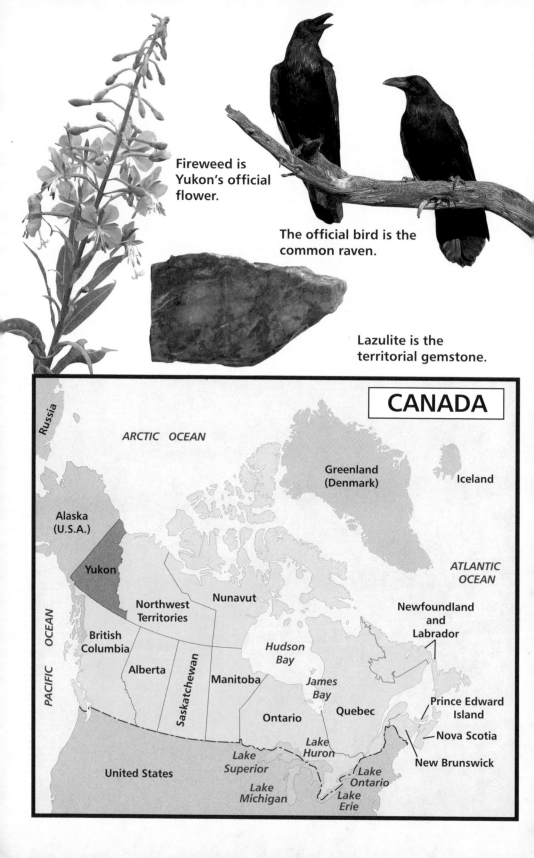

Fireweed is Yukon's official flower.

The official bird is the common raven.

Lazulite is the territorial gemstone.

CANADA

Russia

ARCTIC OCEAN

Greenland (Denmark)

Iceland

Alaska (U.S.A.)

Yukon

Northwest Territories

Nunavut

ATLANTIC OCEAN

Newfoundland and Labrador

PACIFIC OCEAN

British Columbia

Alberta

Saskatchewan

Manitoba

Hudson Bay

James Bay

Quebec

Prince Edward Island

Nova Scotia

Ontario

New Brunswick

United States

Lake Huron

Lake Superior

Lake Michigan

Lake Ontario

Lake Erie

Welcome to Yukon!

Yukon's vast rivers and lakes, valleys, majestic mountains and sprawling arctic **tundra** make it a natural beauty. For well over a century it has attracted adventurers and fortune seekers. When gold was discovered along the Klondike River in 1896, droves of prospectors arrived, hoping to strike it rich in the wild and rugged north. This began Yukon's mining industry, which would lead to the formation of small, far-flung communities.

Today Yukon is proud of its colourful northern traditions. Archaeologists have discovered evidence of the earliest people in North America in Yukon, and relics of the gold rush are on display in museums and as landmarks throughout the territory. The culture of its Aboriginal peoples is being passed down through traditional storytelling and festivals, and in its varied languages.

Let's see what makes Yukon "larger than life."

Chapter 1
Peaks and Plateaus

Yukon, the smallest of Canada's three territories, covers a triangular area of land in the country's northwest corner. It borders the province of British Columbia to the south, the Northwest Territories to the east and the American state of Alaska to the west. The Beaufort Sea, part of the Arctic Ocean, is to the north.

High places

Yukon contains many mountains. The highest are the Saint Elias Mountains in the southwest. Here Canada's tallest peak, Mount Logan, rises to an incredible 5959 metres – and it's still growing! This is because gigantic sections of the Earth's crust, called plates, are continuously crumpling into one another. This process is called tectonic uplifting.

The Saint Elias Mountains block moisture from the Pacific from reaching the interior of the territory. This gives Yukon a dry climate.

Plants and animals

About 60 per cent of Yukon is covered in northern boreal forest, or taiga. Here evergreen trees like spruce and pine grow in abundance. Deciduous trees such as birch and poplar grow in the south. The boreal forest is home to many animals, including caribou, moose, wolves, elk, deer and bears.

North of the **treeline** the growing season is short and the ground is always frozen. Shrubs, flowers and mosses grow here instead of trees.

In the high reaches of Yukon's mountains live 22,000 mountain sheep. Dall's sheep have white coats and large, curled horns. They can be seen perched atop narrow mountain cliffs.

A Dall's sheep

Kluane National Park

You can find glaciers, rivers, forests and eight of Canada's highest mountains in Kluane National Park and Reserve, in the southwest. This park is also home to North America's largest population of grizzly bears. More than 150 species of birds, including bald eagles, can be found here.

The park is especially well-known for its icefields. An icefield is a large area of ice that forms when great amounts of snow fall, **compress** and freeze, eventually turning into ice. The Saint Elias Mountains have the largest non-polar icefield in the world. The ice here is about 700 metres deep!

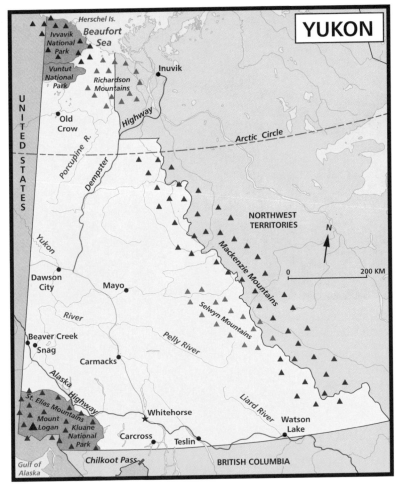

YUKON

Herschel Is.
Beaufort Sea
Ivvavik National Park
Vuntut National Park
UNITED STATES
Richardson Mountains
Inuvik
Old Crow
Porcupine R.
Dempster Highway
Arctic Circle
NORTHWEST TERRITORIES
N
Mackenzie Mountains
0   200 KM
Yukon
Dawson City
Mayo
River
Selwyn Mountains
Pelly River
Beaver Creek
Snag
Carmacks
Alaska Highway
St. Elias Mountains
Mount Logan
Kluane National Park
Whitehorse
Carcross
Teslin
Liard River
Watson Lake
Gulf of Alaska
Chilkoot Pass
BRITISH COLUMBIA

Between 150 and 200 muskoxen live within Ivvavik National Park in the far north.

One-quarter of Canada's grizzly bears live in Yukon. They are found throughout the territory, feeding on fish, roots and berries and occasionally on large animals such as caribou, elk and deer.

Canoeists travel the scenic Yukon River between Whitehorse and Dawson City in summer. The territory was named after this river.

Yukon's interior

The landscape of the Yukon interior is one of rolling uplands cut by deep river systems and interrupted by smaller mountains. The chief plateau of this area is the Yukon Plateau.

The Yukon River, the territory's longest, winds through the interior and into Alaska before draining into the Bering Sea. Many smaller rivers, such as the Teslin, Pelly, White and Stewart feed this massive river system. The Yukon River has served as a transportation route for Aboriginal peoples for centuries, and for European settlers who came later.

More mountains

The mountains in the east are lower than those in the west. They include the Selwyn and Mackenzie Mountains on the border with the Northwest Territories. These are northern extensions of the Rocky Mountains.

The Selwyn Mountains have rounded peaks caused by **glacial erosion**. The British and Richardson Mountains are in the far north. Canada's highest waterfalls and deepest canyons are found here.

A hiker in the Selwyn Mountains

The coastal plain

A narrow strip of tundra stretches for 200 kilometres along the Beaufort Sea. This is the Arctic Coastal Plain. Wetlands cover almost half of this region. Many birds, including snowy owls and raptors, as well as wolves, muskoxen and red fox, are found here.

Pockets of permafrost more than 300 metres deep are scattered throughout this region. Permafrost is frozen ground that never thaws. It stunts the growth of plants because their roots are unable to grow deep enough into the ground. In summer, the top, or active, layer melts, causing pools of water to remain in flat areas. These pools become breeding grounds for countless flies and mosquitoes.

A snowy owl

Polar bears live on the Arctic coast.

On clear winter nights, green, blue and pink ribbons of light stretch across the Yukon sky. These are the aurora borealis, or northern lights.

The midnight sun

Winters are very long and cold in Yukon, with temperatures that can dip to -40 degrees Celsius or lower. Summers are short, but temperatures can soar higher than 30 degrees Celsius. Around December 21 each year, days become very short. During this time, Dawson City only gets about four hours of sunlight a day, Whitehorse gets about six hours, and farther north, the town of Old Crow doesn't get any sunlight at all!

By mid June, twilight remains almost until sunrise. In Old Crow, Yukoners receive an entire 24 hours of sunlight in one day. There is so much sunlight that you can read a book outside at midnight! This is called "the midnight sun."

Mighty Yukon

- With an area of 483,450 square kilometres, Yukon makes up just 4.8 per cent of Canada's total land mass.

- The Yukon River is Canada's second-longest river at 3185 kilometres.

- After Mount McKinley, in Alaska, Mount Logan is the second-highest mountain in North America.

- Beaver Creek is Canada's westernmost community.

- Snag, a village just a few kilometres from Beaver Creek, holds the record for the coldest temperature ever recorded in North America at -63 degrees Celsius!

Mount Logan is Canada's tallest mountain.

Chapter 2
Yukon's Past

Thousands of years ago, when most of North America was covered under great sheets of ice, what is now Alaska was linked to Siberia by a land bridge. This area, called Beringia, was too dry to be covered in ice. Archaeologists believe humans first came to North America this way, by following the mammoths and bison they hunted for food.

Beringia included parts of Yukon. In the Bluefish Caves, in northern Yukon, scientists have found stone tools next to animal bones. This is the earliest evidence of humans in North America – between 15,000 and 20,000 years ago!

Mammoths, like the one illustrated here, are now extinct.

First peoples

Tools carved from the ivory tusks of walruses

With time, many different Aboriginal groups spread throughout Yukon. They lived in small groups, and travelled from place to place with the seasons. In summer they camped by lakes to catch fish with nets, hooks made of animal bone and spears. They used rafts for travelling short distances, and canoes made of cedar and birchbark for long-distance travel.

In fall, larger groups hunted caribou, moose and mountain sheep. Leftover meat was dried for winter, when food would be scarce. In winter, people lived in small groups near lakes, fishing through holes in the ice and snaring smaller animals like beavers, hares and muskrat. When food ran out,

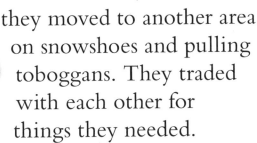

they moved to another area on snowshoes and pulling toboggans. They traded with each other for things they needed.

Bow drills were used for carving, drilling holes and starting fires.

The main Aboriginal groups were the Gwich'in, Han, Kaska, Tagish, Tanana and Tuchone, who spoke different versions of the Na-Dene language. During the 1800s, the Tlingit moved into southern Yukon from the Pacific coast. The Far North was the home and hunting grounds of the Inuvialuit.

Gwich'in moccasins

The fur trade

In the 1800s most of Canada was controlled by the fur trading companies. In the 1840s the Hudson's Bay Company (HBC) sent Robert Campbell to explore the Yukon area. During his eight years here, Campbell set up two HBC forts: Fort Frances in the southeast, and Fort Selkirk on the Yukon River.

Traders with moose antlers on a Yukon river

Arctic explorers were looking for the **Northwest Passage** in the 1800s. In 1825 Sir John Franklin mapped Yukon's Arctic coast.

Fort Selkirk was looted and burned by the Tlingit, who saw the HBC traders as a threat to the trade they had set up between Aboriginal trappers and Russian traders in Alaska. Although more trading posts opened, Aboriginal groups did their best to keep the European fur traders out of their territory.

Changing hands

In 1867 the United States bought Alaska from Russia. Fearing they would also take over the Yukon area, the British government took the land from the HBC and gave it to the newly formed country of Canada. In 1895 the Yukon District was made a part of the Northwest Territories.

Whaling

The Inuvialuit lived and hunted in their territory at Herschel Island in the Beaufort Sea for thousands of years. Each fall, huge numbers of bowhead whales passed by on their yearly migration. The Inuvialuit hunted them for their meat and blubber.

In the late 1800s American whaling ships, loaded with supplies for the winter, arrived in these rich whale-hunting grounds. By the end of the 1800s, about 1500 whalers lived on Herschel Island, making it Yukon's largest community at the time. Overhunting brought the whaling era to an end by 1911. By that time, European diseases and the introduction of alcohol had taken a toll on the Inuvialuit population.

A bowhead whale

American whalers and an Inuvialuit woman, possibly a seamstress, pose on deck at Herschel Island.

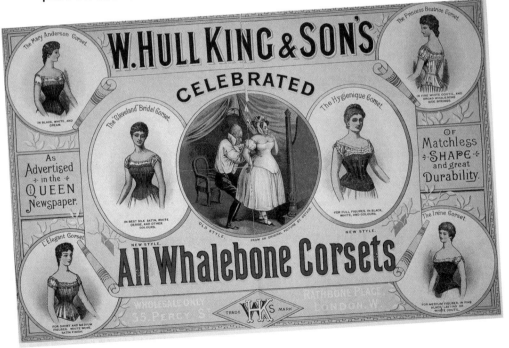

Baleen, or whalebone, was a flexible material used to make ladies' corsets and other items. Whale oil was burned as fuel in some North American cities' street lamps.

Many people with "gold fever" came to Yukon in the late 1890s.

The gold rush

Around 1870, prospectors from the mountains of northern British Columbia started panning the rivers and streams of the Yukon District for gold. In 1896 large gold nuggets were found at Rabbit Creek. Thousands of men and women from Canada, the United States and Europe flooded into the district to seek their fortunes. The Canadian government sent the North West Mounted Police to keep order.

Yukon was made a separate territory on June 13, 1898. Dawson City, the boom town at the heart of the gold rush, was its capital. But within five years, the Klondike Gold Rush was over. It had forever changed Yukon.

Towns had been created and roads had been built. In 1898 over 2000 men, armed with picks and shovels, began construction on a railway between Skagway, Alaska, and Whitehorse, Yukon. The 178-kilometre-long railway was completed in July 1900.

Bust

Many people left Yukon after they failed to strike it rich. **World War I** drew on Yukon's already dwindling population as soldiers went off to the battlefields of Europe. Over 2300 men, more than one-quarter of the population, volunteered before the war ended. In 1901 the population of Yukon had been 27,000. By 1921 it was only about 4000!

Sam Steele is famous as the Mountie who brought order to the territory during the gold rush.

The *Princess Sophia* disaster

In 1918 the steamship *Princess Sophia* sank off the southwest coast of Alaska. It was carrying mail, gold and hundreds of workers leaving Yukon and Alaska for the winter months. Rescue boats tried to save the passengers, but were unable to get close because of strong winds. When the ship sank, all 343 passengers and crew members drowned. Of the victims, 125 people had lived in Dawson City. Almost everyone in Dawson had at least one friend or relative on the *Princess Sophia*.

The *Princess Sophia*

The original Alaska Highway was full of narrow twists and turns. Much of it was constructed on permafrost. When the top layer of ground began to thaw, some sections of the highway sank.

The Alaska Highway

Yukon boomed again during **World War II**. The United States was at war with Japan, and it feared an attack on Alaska. The U.S. government asked the Canadian government if it could build a road to move defensive equipment through Canada to Alaska. The Canadian government agreed. In 1942 highway construction began. About 11,000 American soldiers and 16,000 American and Canadian civilians built the 2400-kilometre road through northern B.C. and Yukon to the Alaska border. It took workers over eight difficult months to complete it.

A photograph of Whitehorse, taken between 1900 and 1903, shows steamboats docked on the Yukon River.

Changing places

The Canol Pipeline, built to move oil from oil fields in the Northwest Territories to a refinery at Whitehorse, also brought workers to Yukon. By 1953 the Yukon population had more than doubled. Whitehorse, which was connected to Alaska by both rail and a highway, became the new capital city.

Land claims

About 20 per cent of the Yukon population is made up of Aboriginal peoples. During the gold rush and the construction of the Alaska Highway, many lost their traditional lands and way of life. Unlike elsewhere in Canada, there were no treaties, or agreements, made between them and the government about land use and ownership. In 1973 they listed their **grievances** with the federal government. After many years of negotiations, a settlement was reached so that 8.5 per cent of the land has been returned to them.

The children of Yukon today

Chapter 3

Striking It Rich

Imagine how excited you'd be if you unearthed a gold nugget – and there was more gold nearby! In August 1896 Californian George Carmack, his Tagish wife Kate, and her brothers Skookum Jim and Dawson Charlie did just that at Rabbit Creek. The creek flowed into a river that the people living in the area called *Throndiuk*. The next day, the gold seekers registered their claims at the community of Forty Mile. As word of their discovery spread, English-speaking people mispronounced the name of the river, calling it Klondike. Thus began the Klondike Gold Rush.

Getting there

The route to gold was dangerous and many people turned back or lost their lives on the journey. Conquering the Chilkoot Pass required trekking up about 1500 steps cut into deep snow on a steep mountainside. The North West Mounted Police (NWMP) set up posts at the summit. They ensured that tax was paid on goods brought into Yukon, and that all gold seekers had a year's worth of supplies with them. It took each person about 30 trips to bring all of these goods to the top. They carried them on their backs and on animals, as well as on sleds.

Prospectors were required by the NWMP to take 1000 kilograms of goods with them to Dawson City. These included boots, lamps, tools such as picks and shovels, and food such as beans, tea and sugar.

At the summit, the prospectors reached the shore of Lindeman Lake, but they still had to travel almost 800 kilometres by water to reach Dawson City, the settlement closest to the gold. To cross the lake and sail up the Yukon River, they had to make their own simple boats or rafts. These had to be strong enough to carry passengers and supplies and to withstand the river's rapids. To make them, the prospectors cut down trees around Lindeman Lake.

Gold seekers struggled in single file up and over Chilkoot Pass. Those who slipped and fell, or stopped to rest, would lose their place in line.

Prospectors panned for gold in the creeks and streams near the Klondike. They used shallow pans and shook them to separate the gold pieces from dirt and gravel.

Today tourists can hike the Chilkoot Trail, where they can still see belongings, like rusty pots, stoves and these boots, that gold seekers abandoned along the way.

Prospectors visited the saloons and gambling halls of Dawson City. The city was called "The Paris of the North."

Dawson City

Those who survived reached Dawson City – by 1898 a bustling town of more than 30,000 people. When they got there, many were disappointed to find that most of the claims had already been staked out. Some headed for home, while others stayed and made a fortune providing goods and services to miners. Dawson City became the largest city north of San Francisco and west of Winnipeg. Along the banks of the Klondike River, a tributary of the Yukon, 500 buildings sprang up. These included theatres, restaurants, a bank, churches and general stores. Street vendors sold French champagnes, parasols, porcelain and delicacies imported from Europe.

Cancan dancers kick up their heels in a restored Dawson City casino.

Writing about the Klondike

The mad dash for Yukon gold inspired many people to write about what was going on in the north. Laura Beatrice Berton wrote an autobiography called *I Married the Klondike*. Her desire to write about life during the gold rush was passed down to her son, Pierre Berton. He grew up in Dawson City and

wrote many books about the gold rush. One of them, *Klondike*, recounts the difficult journey to Dawson City, and the fascinating life there.

Robert Service was a bank clerk and poet who lived in Dawson City from 1909 to 1912. He is most famous for his story poems "The Cremation of Sam McGee" and "The Shooting of Dan McGrew."

Chapter 4
Mining, Trapping and Tourism

The government is the biggest employer in the Yukon today. About one-third of Yukoners work in jobs such as social services, health care and education.

Mining and exploration

Although most famous for its gold supply, Yukon also has major deposits of **tungsten**, zinc, silver, coal, copper and lead. Some of the world's largest deposits of iron ore and zinc can be found in Yukon. Many of the territory's communities are centred around mines.

Today machines are used to mine for gold from rivers.

Celebrating Yukon's gold rush history is a big draw for tourists. Here, entrants from around the world compete at gold panning.

Larger than life

Tourism is the territory's largest industry. More than 300,000 people from around the world visit Yukon each year. About 70 per cent of Yukoners work in jobs related to tourism, including transportation, food services, retail and recreation. Tourists come to Yukon to visit its parks, such as Vuntut National Park and Kluane National Park and Reserve. They paddle up Yukon's lakes and rivers in canoes and kayaks, hike, climb mountain peaks and try dogsledding.

Despite the cold, people enjoy spending time outdoors in winter.

An oat field at harvest time near Whitehorse

Agriculture

Most of Yukon is unsuitable for farming, so agriculture is a small industry here. Farms in the southwest grow crops such as hay and vegetables. Cattle, sheep, chicken and pigs are raised on some livestock farms.

Fishing

'mon

Fishing is an important source of income for many families, and commercial fisheries can be found throughout the territory. Freshwater fish such as salmon and steelhead are caught using gill nets. These mesh nets are stretched across streams or rivers, and the fish become stuck by the gills in the holes of the mesh. Much of the freshwater catch is dried and smoked, and sold locally. Commercial fisheries also harvest fish, including lake trout, whitefish and salmon, to be sold to other countries.

A traditional salmon trap at Klukshu Village, near Kluane National Park in the southwest

Trapping

The fur trade is the territory's oldest industry. Today trappers sell the pelts of fox, muskrat, beaver and wolverine. They normally earn the most money from the sale of marten and lynx pelts, although the prices they receive for the pelts depend on the demand for them. In recent years, the worldwide demand for fur has decreased, which has lowered the income of trappers.

Fox pelts for sale

Martens are members of the weasel family. They are easy for trappers to catch because of their curious nature.

Whaling

The Inuvialuit still hunt whales today, but the hunt is regulated by Fisheries and Oceans Canada. Whale meat is commercially sold through shops and supermarkets, mostly in northern communities where it is part of the traditional diet. Marine **conservationists** are concerned that the continued hunting of whales will lead to their extinction.

Whalers carve up a bowhead whale.

Chapter 5
Life on the Land

Just over 33,000 people live in Yukon. About three-quarters of the population live in Whitehorse, Yukon's capital and largest city. The next largest centres are Dawson City and Watson Lake. The population of many communities has risen and fallen with the boom and bust times. Boom mining towns like Elsa and Keno are now tiny historic villages.

An aerial photograph of Whitehorse, the capital of Yukon

Main Street in Whitehorse

Getting around

Although most Yukon communities are connected by roads, snowmobiles are a popular means of winter transportation. Dogsledding and snowshoeing are the traditional ways to travel on snow.

Yukon Quest

The Yukon Quest is a 1600–kilometre sled dog race held every February. The starting location alternates between Whitehorse, in Yukon, and Fairbanks, in Alaska. Teams of up to fourteen sled dogs and one musher race along a route that runs over frozen rivers, through four mountain ranges, across open water and past northern communities. For most teams, the race takes between ten and fourteen days to complete.

Artist Ted Harrison painted Yukon scenes in bold colours. He lived and taught art in the territory for many years.

Old Crow

Yukon's northernmost community is Old Crow. It is 130 kilometres north of the Arctic Circle. There are no roads to get here. The only way is by plane or boat.

The small town is made up of about 300 people, most of whom belong to the Vuntut Gwich'in group. It is important to the residents to keep Gwich'in traditions alive. They live in log homes, and fish, trap and hunt, particularly the Porcupine caribou herd, for food, shelter, medicines and clothing. Each family in Old Crow has its own trapping area that has been passed down over several generations.

Today some people still choose to live "off the land," as this traditional hunting camp shows.

Meat and more

Meat is the main ingredient in traditional Yukon cooking. Because of the short growing season, few fruit and vegetable farms can survive here. Instead, food has to be brought in from farther south, and this makes the price high.

Moose and caribou are two of the most popular meats. Traditionally, every part of an animal that was killed for food was used in some way. Even the animals' organs are eaten, in dishes such as stuffed caribou heart. Other meats include mountain goat, muskox, hare and porcupine.

Different kinds of berries grow wild in Yukon. Some of the most common for eating are crowberries, cranberries, raspberries and blueberries.

Cranberries and blueberries

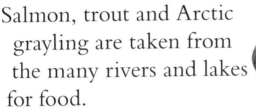

Salmon, trout and Arctic grayling are taken from the many rivers and lakes for food.

During the gold rush, miners brought sourdough – a fermented flour and water mixture – with them to the Klondike. They slept with their sourdough because, if it froze, it was no good for making bread. Yukon old-timers are sometimes referred to as sourdoughs.

Totem poles carved by the Tlingit people stand in front of a heritage centre in Teslin.

Chapter 6
Points of Pride

▶ Mount Churchill erupted twice about 2000 years ago, blanketing 340,000 square kilometres of Yukon and the Northwest Territories with volcanic ash. Layers of ash up to 60 centimetres thick lie beneath the surface of the Alaska Highway.

▶ In the town of Watson Lake grows the famous Sign Post Forest. Carl Lindley, an American soldier working on building the Alaska Highway, erected the first sign in 1942. It pointed to his faraway hometown of Danville, Illinois, and marked the distance. Soon after, others began adding their own signs. Today there are more than 64,000 signs from around the world.

▶ The Dempster Highway is a 671-kilometre road that connects Yukon to the Northwest Territories. It was named after NWMP officer William John Duncan Dempster, who patrolled the route by dogsled. It is Canada's only public route that crosses the Arctic Circle. In winter, the highway extends another 194 kilometres over frozen areas of the Mackenzie River **delta**.

▶ Audrey McLaughlin was the first woman and Yukoner to lead a national political party. She was the New Democratic Party leader from 1989 to 1995.

▶ Elijah Smith was a chief of the Whitehorse Indian Band, now Kwanlin Dün First Nation. In 1973 he presented *Together Today for Our Children Tomorrow*, a document that sparked the Aboriginal **land claims** movement.

Glossary

compresses: Becomes denser by pressure

conservationists: People who work to protect forests, wildlife or natural resources for future use

delta: A triangular area of earth and sand deposited at the mouth of a river

glacial erosion: The wearing down and removal of rocks and soil by a glacier – a mass of slow-moving, compacted snow and ice

grievances: Official complaints of injustice

land claims: Legal declarations of desired control over areas

Northwest Passage: A water route through the Canadian Arctic from the Atlantic Ocean to the Pacific Ocean

treeline: The northern limit beyond which no trees grow

tundra: A treeless arctic plain

tungsten: A silvery-grey metal used in electronic parts

World War I: An international conflict (1914-1918) that took place largely in Europe, and in which an estimated ten million lives were lost

World War II: An international conflict (1939-1945) that spread throughout Europe, North Africa, southeast Asia and the western Pacific, and claimed the lives of an estimated 55 million people